The Secret Service, originally formed to fight counterfeiters, once cracked down on a Philadelphia baker for his cookies designed to look like pennies.

The Bank of England once protected itself against highway robbery by ripping its banknotes in half and sending them in two separate shipments.

The underground vaults at Fort Knox are so secure that not even an atomic blast could penetrate their walls.

The cost of Columbus's discovery of America came to about $7,000, financed by Queen Isabella who used her jewels as collateral to obtain a loan.

YOU CAN'T COUNT A BILLION DOLLARS

& OTHER LITTLE-KNOWN FACTS ABOUT MONEY

Barbara Seuling

IVY BOOKS • NEW YORK

The author wishes to thank the American Numismatic Society for its help during the research for this book.

Ivy Books
Published by Ballantine Books
Copyright © 1979, 1991 by Barbara Seuling

Library of Congress Catalog Card Number: 78-22354

ISBN 0-8041-0657-6

Manufactured in the United States of America

First Ballantine Books Edition: June 1991

To the memory of my brother
Phil Seuling,
who would have tried it

1

HALF-PENNIES AND ONE-CENT NICKELS

○   The first coins were bean-shaped pellets made in the Greek state of Lydia in about 600 B.C. They were made from a natural mixture of gold and silver called electrum, found in local riverbeds.

○   The temples of gods and goddesses were the first Greek mints. Coins were stamped with images or symbols of the divine beings in whose temples they were made. One coin, bearing the engraving of an owl, which was the symbol of Athens, took about two months to make.

○ A Chinese coin struck early in the Tang Dynasty (A.D. 618–907) introduced the practice of inscribing coins. The theory is that by accident the Empress's fingernail made an impression in the wax mold, and the impression kept being repeated because no one dared to change it.

○ A sculpture known as the "Winged Victory of Samothrace" was reconstructed in recent times mainly from the images on coins issued in about 300 B.C.

○ The Carthaginians and ancient Romans used money that was made of leather.

○ Some ancient coins were shaped like hams.

○ The first silver coins minted were based upon the values of sheep.

○ In A.D. 1260, Louis IX of France had no coins in his treasury to pay his troops, and there was no time to mint new ones, so he invented an emergency coin made of a small piece of silver wire snipped off and fastened to a square of leather stamped with its value. These are the coins the troops received for their wages.

○ In 1544, Henry VIII of England was nicknamed "Old Coppernose," after he issued a poor-quality shilling from which the silver could be rubbed off.

○ Money, which was once in the form of objects that could be weighed, explains how the English pound got its name; it first referred to a load of 7,680 dried grains of wheat.

○ Coins were once cut into pieces to make change. That's how Great Britain got her halfpenny and farthings . . . originally known as "fourthings," or fourths of a penny. Similarly, Americans adopted the term "two bits" for a quarter of a dollar from the Spanish dollar, which was divided into eight parts, or bits.

○ The American colonies were desperate for coins before the Revolution and used any that they could get their hands on—French, English, Spanish, Portuguese, etc. Even with the variety of coins, few remained in the colonies, as the settlers sent them abroad to purchase supplies for building new homes.

○ When the colonists finally struck their own coins, the dollar was adopted as the unit of U.S. money, based on the Spanish dollar, the most popular currency in pre-Revolutionary America.

○ The first coins in the American colonies were called "Pine Tree Shillings" for their design and were produced in Boston in 1652.

○ The first coin bearing the name of the United States of America was the Fugio cent of 1787. It bore the motto "Mind Your Business."

○ George Washington did not want his portrait on United States coins. The symbol of Liberty was used instead until many years later when Washington's profile appeared on the quarter.

○ Portraits of living persons on American coins are extremely rare.

○ Nobody knows for sure how the dollar sign came to be. Some say it is the roughly written initials of the country: U.S. Others say that it is a rough form of the figure eight, for the eight-part Spanish dollar on which the American dollar is based. Some people believe that our dollar sign is a modification of the English symbol for the pound: £. The most generally accepted theory is that it is a symbol from the early Phoenicians, signifying strength and sovereignty.

○ In 1792 the first official U.S. Mint was established in Philadelphia. Metals for minting the first coins were scarce, and colonists donated old nails, spikes, finishings from old or wrecked ships, and kitchen utensils. It is recorded that George Washington donated his wife Martha's "excellent copper teakettle as well as two pairs of tongs" to the cause.

○ The budget of the first U.S. Mint, apparently excluding employee wages, was as follows:

Property purchase	$4,266.67
Straw, hay, and horse medicine	2.00
Director's salary	2,000.00
Watchdog	3.00
Yard alarm bell	17.82
120 bushels of coal	38.00
Six pounds old copper	1.00

○ The first U.S. Mint was closed only for the Fourth of July and Christmas, unless there was a yellow fever epidemic, in which case it was closed for months at a time. Workers at the Mint had to bring their lunch from home—they were not allowed to go out. Once they arrived at 5:00 A.M., they were not allowed to leave until 8:00 P.M.—quitting time. Only the night watchman could feed the watchdog.

○ When the first U.S. Mint was in operation, a citizen could lawfully bring silver and gold to the Mint to be made into U.S. coins, free of charge.

○ There was once a one-cent nickel. In 1857 the large copper cent was changed to a new alloy of 88 percent copper and 12 percent nickel. It was called the nickel cent, which gave way to the nickname "nickel."

○ From 1875 to 1878, the United States had a coin in the denomination of twenty cents.

○ In the early twentieth century, a U.S. dollar contained 23.22 grains of pure gold.

○ In 1919, after World War I, Germany was bankrupt and manufactured coins from any available materials ... cardboard, glass, porcelain, clay, even cloth. By 1923 the cloth money had been embellished by the addition of lace edgings and fancy needlework.

○ The province of Kweichow, in the Republic of China, produced a silver dollar in 1928 which is probably the only coin in the world to use the automobile as part of its design.

○ The buffalo depicted on the 1938 buffalo nickel was "Black Diamond," from the Bronx Zoo in New York City.

○ In 1943 a zinc-coated steel penny was produced in the United States so that the more precious metal, copper, normally used in pennies, could be used for the war effort.

○ Until 1965 our U.S. silver coinage was almost unchanged, but in 1964 there was a coin shortage in which the silver dollar, the Kennedy half-dollar and the wartime nickel of the 1940s had almost completely disappeared from circulation. The cause was blamed, among other things, on the proliferation of coin collectors and vending machines. The silver shortage caused the removal of silver from dimes and quarters and reduced it in half-dollars. In 1970, it was removed from half-dollars and dollars as well.

○ Once a coin is designed and adopted, it may not be changed for at least twenty-five years without special legislation.

○ Some famous coin collectors have included the Roman Emperor Augustus, France's Charlemagne, Austria's Empress Maria Theresa, and King George II of England.

○ A single stamping machine can produce coins at the rate of 10,000 per hour.

2

TREE BARK AND TWO-DOLLAR BILLS

○ Paper money is an invention of the Chinese. When Marco Polo visited the great emperor Kublai Khan, he noted that money was printed on the pressed bark of the mulberry tree and stamped with the Great Khan's seal. No one dared not accept the notes.

○ In India the one-rupee note has the denomination written out in thirteen different dialects.

◯   The first American paper money was printed by the colony of Massachusetts in 1690 to pay soldiers. Coins were hard to come by, so paper money was instituted, and each state issued its own.

◯   When England prohibited the printing of paper money by the colonies in 1764, the Americans defiantly went on printing it. Patriot Paul Revere issued some in Massachusetts. The money, called "continentals," kept losing value because there was nothing to support it, but it helped win the Revolutionary War. Nobody in Europe could figure out just how much money the colonies had, and it confused them.

◯   In the Virginia and Maryland colonies, tobacco was used as money during the seventeenth and eighteenth centuries.

○ The smallest size paper money ever produced was the Hong Kong one-cent note, issued during World War II as an emergency measure when they ran out of coins.

○ The paper used in U.S. paper money is specially made by Crane & Company of Dalton, Massachusetts, who has been the sole supplier of the special paper since 1879. It is a blend of rag bond, cotton, and linen. No wood pulp—the basis of most ordinary paper—is used. It is illegal for anyone else to make this paper, and the formula is kept secret. None has ever been stolen, because it is so carefully guarded. If a sheet is found to be defective, it cannot be just thrown away. It must be sent through various departments for cancellation, scheduling, verification, and finally, destruction.

○ A money bill goes through the printing press three times. Once it is printed on the front in black. Then it is printed on the back in green. Then the front is "overprinted" in light green ink, showing the serial numbers and the Treasury Department seal.

○   If an asterisk appears in front of the serial number on a dollar bill, it means that the original bill was defective, and this one replaced it. The defect was noted after the printing of the serial number.

○   The life expectancy of a dollar bill is about eighteen months.

○   In 1916 dirty paper money was sent to Washington to be laundered. If the money was found to be in good condition, it was washed, ironed, and reissued, saving the government a few hundred dollars a day in printing costs.

○ The first and only U.S. paper currency to bear the portrait of a woman was the one-dollar silver certificate issued in 1886. The woman portrayed was Martha Washington.

○ Before 1929 U.S. paper money was one-third larger than it is today. It was referred to as "saddle blankets."

○ By law, no living person can be portrayed on a money bill of the United States.

○   The design of paper money is the responsibility of the Secretary of the Treasury.

○   The denominations of paper money in use today in the United States are the $1, $2, $5, $10, $20, $50, and $100 bills. Bigger bills are printed but used only in bank transactions and not released to the public.

○   There are still more than 300 ten-thousand dollar bills in circulation, although they have not been printed since 1944.

○   If a money bill is damaged but three-fifths of it is still in good condition, it can be redeemed at full face value. If less than three-fifths remains, but more than two-fifths, it can be redeemed for half the face value. If less than two-fifths remains, it is worthless.

○ It would take 257,588,120 U.S. dollar bills, laid
end to end, to circle the earth at the equator.

○ A billion, in the United States, is considered to
be a thousand million and is written like this:

$$1,000,000,000$$

In Great Britain, it is considered a million million,
which is written like this:

$$1,000,000,000,000$$

Therefore, if you counted approximately 150 bills a
minute and worked sixteen hours a day—leaving
the other eight for eating and sleeping—it would
take you twenty years to count a billion dollars
United States style. If you did it English style, it
would be impossible. It would take 19,025 years.

○ Some banks in Wales issued their own private bank notes in the nineteenth century, printed with pictures of sheep, since many of their customers could not read.

○ Following World War II, a Swiss soap manufacturer bought worthless Austrian paper kronen notes which had lost their monetary value because of postwar inflation and wrapped soap in them.

○ When a devil's face appeared in the folds of the Queen's hair on a Canadian bank note issued in 1954, the public would not handle the notes, and they had to be withdrawn. No one knows whether it was accidental or deliberate on the part of the engraver.

3

FAKES AND FORGERS

○ There is evidence that counterfeiters have been practicing their craft since about the fourth century B.C.

○ The crime of counterfeiting was taken very seriously among the ancients. Counterfeiters in China could have their hands—or their heads—cut off. In Rome, a freeman could have his taxes waived for life if he reported a counterfeiter. A slave could secure his freedom. And if a counterfeiter escaped from jail, his jailer could be executed.

○ Historians believe that Charles IX of France was an excellent counterfeiter. He and his supporters flooded the country with imitation enemy coinage in order to force the enemy's economy to decline.

○ Coin clipping was a common practice in medieval times. Coin makers and handlers of large amounts of coins would clip the edges off coins, save up the clippings, and make new coins with the shavings. The practice was once so widespread in England that all coin makers were summoned before the king, and those who could not prove that they had not clipped coins had their right hands cut off.

○ Sometimes the edges of coins were imprinted with a motto to discourage clipping. In Oliver Cromwell's time, the inscription around English coins read: THE PENALTY FOR CLIPPING THIS COIN IS DEATH.

○   The first currency to be counterfeited in the colonies was wampum, made of shells and beads, which served as money for colonists as well as native Indians. The Indians counterfeited some wampum passed to the white man by dying white shells bluish black; darker-colored shells were more valuable.

○   The practice of transporting criminals to the colonies was a common English practice. One shipload arrived in Maryland in 1770, and within a few days, counterfeit money had already appeared.

○   There were several women counterfeiters in the thirteen colonies—two in Connecticut, one in New Hampshire, and seven in Pennsylvania.

○ During the French Revolution, the Bank of England, with the approval of the British government, was involved in forgery when it created fake French assignat notes.

○ In the early 1800s hundreds of forgers were hanged on the gallows each year in England. Famous artist George Cruikshank drew a caricature of an English bank note, showing some criminals hanging by the neck and British ships carrying other criminals to exile in the British colonies. The drawing was published, and the resulting publicity led to the abolition of the death penalty for so minor a crime.

○ To make it harder for counterfeiters, South Carolina printed Hebrew and Greek letters on its paper money in 1776.

○ During the early part of the Civil War, about a third of all currency in circulation in the country was counterfeit. President Abraham Lincoln ordered that a permanent force be set up to stop the rampant counterfeiting problem during his administration. The force became the Secret Service.

○ In its early days, the Secret Service was so diligent that it stopped a Philadelphia baker from baking cookies designed like United States pennies.

○ Counterfeiter J. B. Cross, while serving a term in prison, forged his own pardon from the Governor of Pennsylvania. Only a technicality in how the pardon was presented to prison authorities kept Cross from getting away with it.

○ Counterfeit detectors find phony bills by the use of ultraviolet rays, which pick up the whiteners used in the manufacture of most papers as a bright glow. Other detectors are set up to "read" one or two places on a bill, for use in money-changing machines.

○ The ink used on United States paper money contains ferric oxide, which has magnetic properties. Some counterfeit detectors pick up signals given off by this ingredient.

○ At a German concentration camp during World War II, several hundred prisoners who were excellent forgers were forced to prepare the plates for counterfeit British bank notes, U.S. dollars, and French franc notes.

○ During a severe coin shortage in 1964, many banks and small businesses devised ways to help out. A bank in Wisconsin produced wooden nickels which local merchants agreed to accept as small change, but the Treasury Department forced them to stop because they could be considered as counterfeit U.S. currency.

4

CURIOUS CUSTOMS

○ The famous biblical sale, in which Esau sold his birthright for a "bowl of pottage," was probably for a pot of lentils.

○ The ancient Chinese offered sacrifices regularly to Ts'ai-shen, the god of wealth. The ancient Greeks considered the god Hermes, known mainly as the runner, also as the god of profit.

○ The word "cash" comes from the Chinese word "kasu," meaning small coin. The word "money" comes from ancient Rome, where the goddess Juno Moneta stood guard over the temple where coins were minted. The Byzantine solidus, a gold coin used to pay soldiers, gave us our word "soldier." And our word "salary" comes from "salarias," which is the name of payments made in salt to Roman soldiers under Julius Caesar.

○ The first container which was used for money was probably a money bag, or saccus, according to references in ancient Greek and Roman writings.

○ Coins were once placed on corpses, or on their graves, to ensure that the deceased would be able to pay the boatman's fare when he was ferried over to the land of the dead.

○ The Chinese issued "hell money," which was fake paper money to be buried with corpses. They believed that the spirit would need money in the next world.

○ The term "pin money" comes from a custom in Queen Elizabeth I's time, when, during a kind of annual shopping spree for the Queen, her ladies-in-waiting got a bonus for themselves. Many of the ladies spent their extra money on a new invention—metal pins.

○ At dances in colonial America, gentlemen danced with ladies in the order of their wealth. The most important male guest danced with the richest girl first, then the second richest, and so on.

○ In colonial times, the scarf was a purse worn around the neck.

○ Every year, natives of the Duke of York Islands in the South Pacific decorate a canoe with green leaves, load it with money, and set it adrift to "pay" the fish for those of their relatives that were caught.

○ Some people used coins to close the eyelids of a corpse. It is believed that the doctor attending President Lincoln at his death closed his eyes with silver dollars.

○   It was once a crime punishable by three months' imprisonment for an Englishman who earned less than £20 a year to wear silk in his nightcap. In the American colonies, only persons with more than £200 could wear gold or silver lace or buttons, or any lace costing more than two shillings a yard.

○ In India, some cakes are frosted with thin sheets of real gold, which is eaten along with the cake.

○ A man in Cameroon can buy a bride with "wife money," small spears about thirty inches long. It takes about a dozen of these to make a purchase.

○ The word "tip" is said to come from the letters T.I.P., which stand for "To Insure Promptness."

○ The soap operas most popular in England feature lower- and lower-middle-class characters, while the American favorites feature well-to-do professionals, millionaires, and tycoons.

○ The U.S. Treasury Department has a "conscience fund," set up by President James Madison in 1811. Any time an American citizen sends "conscience" money to the government, to make up for equipment taken while in the army, for underpaying taxes, etc., it goes into this fund. About a quarter of a million dollars is added to the fund each year.

5

IT'S A LIVING

○ Dealing in mummies in medieval times was a profitable business. European physicians used bitumen to cure many ailments, and it was believed that mummies in Egypt were wrapped in linens which had been soaked in this substance. Tombs were robbed, mummies unwound, and the linens reduced to powder and sold. As the demand grew, whole mummies were powdered and shipped instead of just the wrappings.

○ Alchemists, who were sort of medieval chemists, scientists, and astrologers all rolled into one, spent much of their time trying to find the formula for turning base metals into pure gold.

○   Rembrandt, whose paintings are now valued at millions of dollars apiece, was so broke in his lifetime that in 1657 the Insolvency Office of Amsterdam had to auction all his possessions in order to pay off his debts.

○   During his years as a general in the American Revolutionary War, George Washington paid his own expenses. Congress reimbursed him after the war.

○   A private in the Continental Army earned about twenty-five pence, or fifty-two cents, a month.

○ Benjamin Franklin thought that the president of the United States should receive no salary because it would become a corruptive influence.

○ In the nineteenth century, body-snatching was a thriving business. Bodies were sold by the shipload to medical schools for anatomical study. An adult corpse sold for about four English pounds. Children's bodies were sold by the inch.

○ Macy's, the world's largest department store, earned about $11 on its first day of business in 1858.

○   The Pullman car, with its unique sleeping facilities, was not a success in the United States until the death of Abraham Lincoln, when the state of Illinois bought one of the cars for the president's funeral train. From that time on, Pullman cars grew in popularity and were a financial success.

○   Sigmund Freud's most important work, *The Interpretation of Dreams*, now in print and studied all over the world, paid the author only $209 when it was published in 1899 and took eight years to sell out a printing of 600 copies.

○   When Thomas Edison learned that his company was making defective batteries in 1905, he paid a million dollars out of his own pocket to give refunds to buyers.

○ The author of "Casey at the Bat," a famous poem often recited, received only a $5.00 flat fee for it.

○ An inventor named Dr. Plimpton earned a million dollars for his famous invention—roller skates.

○ A law in Arkansas states that schoolteachers who bob their hair will not get a raise.

○ Artist Claude Monet's career got started when he won 100,000 francs in the state lottery and became financially independent. Monet's work is now among the most valuable in the art world.

○   According to a well-known financial organiza-
tion, a child under six years old should be given
enough allowance to pay for his or her own candy,
gum, ice cream, small toys, gifts for others, books,
playthings, paints, crayons, blocks, and dolls.

○   George Bush, as president of the United States,
receives a salary of $200,000 plus expenses. The first
president, George Washington, received $25,000
and had to pay his own expenses.

○   An average rock star gets paid around four cents
for every single record sold and about twenty-five
cents for each LP.

○ Among the ten most boring jobs in the country, according to polls, are those of bank guards and highway toll takers—both occupations involving money.

○ In 1981, an early self-portrait by artist Pablo Picasso was sold at auction for $5,300,000.

○   Artist Andy Warhol said that when he was searching for a subject for his art, a friend suggested he focus on what he loved the most—and he started painting money.

6

SECURITIES AND INSECURITIES

○ Writing checks is not a modern idea. Checks were inscribed on clay tablets in ancient Babylonia and used as currency.

○ There is evidence that around 3,000 B.C., Babylonian temples were depositories for money and places where loans were made.

○ Cleopatra bet her lover, Mark Antony, that she could drink $500,000 worth of wine without leaving the table. Antony accepted the bet, and she dropped two valuable pearls into a glass of wine and drank them down.

○ Julius Caesar, who sought to increase the population of Rome, offered rewards to his soldiers for having many children.

○ In the early fourteenth century, bankers from northern Italy introduced money-lending into London. Several of England's kings were financed by their services.

○   The Bank of England once issued bisected bank notes—paper currency cut in half—to protect shipments of money to their branch offices. Each shipment contained only half of the money, so that highway robbers intercepting shipments would gain nothing.

○   The first loan taken out by the new United States Government was made on September 13, 1789, in order to pay the salaries of the president and members of Congress. The money was borrowed from the Bank of New York and the Bank of North America, at 6 percent interest.

○   There were no banks in the colonies before the American Revolution. If you wanted to borrow money, you had to go to an individual for a loan.

○   Highwaymen of the eighteenth century were also known as "gentlemen of the road." Mostly from respectable homes, they resorted to robbery when their inheritances ran out or they lost their fortunes in gambling. Others had served as footmen to wealthy employers and had learned the habits of luxury, which only money illegally obtained could maintain.

○ The piggy bank is not named after the pig but after a kind of clay. Almost every home once had kitchen utensils made of a common clay known as pygg. Money was often kept in a household pot or jug made of this material, and these containers came to be called pygg banks, or pyggy banks.

○ Gertrude Stein and her brother Leo were the only ones who wanted Picasso's work when he was a young painter in Paris and bought their first painting from him for about thirty dollars. They continued to collect his work, which grew to be among the most valuable in the art world.

○ The first life insurance policy came about when some men convinced a fellow in a bar into paying them eighty dollars, and if he died within the year, they would pay his widow two hundred dollars. The man died, and a court upheld the contract.

◯   The first person to receive Social Security payments was a woman, Ida M. Fuller of Ludlow, Vermont, who received check number 00-000-001 for $22.54 on January 31, 1940.

◯   An actor named Conrad Cantzen left a fund of $227,000 so that any professional actor with run-down shoes may apply at the Actors Equity office and receive a trip to the shoe store for a new pair of shoes.

◯   Lloyd's of London, famous for insuring almost any risk for a price, has insured Jimmy Durante's nose, Fred Astaire's legs, and the airship Hindenburg.

O   The insurance on men's jewelry costs about twice as much as that on women's jewelry because men are found to be less careful about jewelry than women.

O   The odds on winning the Irish sweepstakes are 450,000 to 1. The odds against the jackpot (three bars) coming up on a slot machine are 8,000 to 1.

O   Credit cards can be used to pay for just about anything: tombstones, diamonds, apartment rent, music lessons, church donations, college tuition, psychiatric care, marriage fees, taxes, and in Nevada, you can post bail with one.

○ The average American carries $27 in his wallet, according to *Money* magazine.

○ Zoologist Desmond Morris studied the "profit motive" in apes. He gave them crayons and paints, and they made interesting pictures. Then he gave them peanuts as "payment" for their drawings and paintings, and they began scribbling any old thing just to get the reward.

○ Hong Kong has more banks per square mile than almost any other place in the world.

○ The currency vault in Fort Knox, Kentucky, built by the United States government in 1936 to hold its store of gold bullion, has underground vaults so secure that they cannot be penetrated even by an atomic blast.

○ The Federal Reserve Bank in New York City houses the world's largest store of gold. Every grain of gold that goes into the bank must be accounted for. Workers who enter the vaults in which the gold is stored in bricklike fashion have to wear special protective shoes designed to protect themselves as well as the gold.

○ Americans save only 4.6 percent of their income; the Japanese put away 17.2 percent for a rainy day.

7
STONES AND BONES

○ Shells are probably the oldest form of money in the world. The most valuable shells are those of the cowrie, a sea snail with a colorful shell. The rarest of these is the white-toothed variety, of which only two are known to exist.

○ In China, money started out as symbols of the objects, such as spades and knives, which were once used in trade. Some say that the hole that still appears in the Chinese yen today is a leftover from the time when such "knife money" had a hole in the handle, probably for stringing the tokens together.

○   The Japanese once used "tree money," which consisted of coins that could be broken from "branches" as needed to make change.

○   In ancient Egypt, bread was used as currency and even appears as payment on an ancient payroll. Pictures of royal bakeries were included in the elaborate murals in the tombs of pharaohs to show their wealth.

○   Barley was the first acceptable form of money used in Mesopotamia. Cattle were used as money in early Rome.

○ When knights returned home from crusades in medieval times, they counted beans among the most valuable treasures brought home from the East.

○ In the Middle Ages, pepper was a highly valued spice. Many European cities became wealthy due to the importation of pepper. Taxes could be paid with it, and soldiers were often rewarded for their victories with bonuses of the spice.

○ The Spanish conquerors of Mexico in the sixteenth century found the treasure houses of the Aztec Indians filled more with mountains of cacao beans than with gold or silver. The beans were prized for their food value and were used as currency throughout Central America.

○ In 1572 the town of Leyden, Holland, was under siege, and money disappeared, along with household silver, as people hoarded their valuables. In order to have currency for everyday trade, the town took its books from the town library, tore out the pages, glued several together, and stamped them as if they were metal. After the siege the "book money" was redeemed, and the town's library was started over again from scratch.

○ In seventeenth-century Canada, playing cards were once issued in place of money. Money from France had not arrived in time to pay French soldiers stationed there, so the cards served temporarily.

○ Gizzi pennies, long twisted rods of iron used as money by a tribe of West Africa, serve as money only while they remain unbroken. If they break, the "soul" is believed to have escaped. Only the tribe's high priest can fix a penny. For a small fee, he solders the two pieces together again.

○ The coastal Indians of North America used shell money known as wampum. Holes were bored in the shells, and they were polished, strung, and made into belts. White settlers as well as Indians used wampum in exchange for goods until 1760, when a man named Campbell decided to mass produce it. He built a factory, complete with machines for drilling and polishing, in what is now Hackensack, New Jersey. The wholesale production of wampum rapidly caused it to become worthless.

○ Dried codfish was used as money in Newfoundland in colonial days. Sugar served as money in the West Indies. Tobacco was legal tender in the South. Iron nails were used as small change in colonial times and were so highly prized that a man might burn down his house to recover the nails for building a new one.

○ On an island called Yap in the South Pacific, the heaviest money in the world can be found. It is in the odd form of great stone wheels, some as small as dinner plates, some twelve feet across. The wheels are cut from limestone, quarried from an island 400 miles distant, and brought back on rafts. Yap chiefs own the largest stones and stand them by their doorways to show off their wealth and importance. An average man looking for a wife can trade a thirty-inch wheel for one, and a six-foot wheel is worth a whole village.

○   On Santa Cruz Island, northeast of Australia, natives still use bird feathers as currency. They weave the exotic red plumage of the honey eater into coils or belts, which are then interchangeable for goods.

○   Hard-packed tea leaves, pressed into bricks, are used as currency in Tibet, Mongolia, and some parts of Siberia.

○ Soap was once used as money in Mexico, remaining valuable only as long as the stamping of the town's name could still be read.

○ Other objects that have served as money at various times around the world are: slaves, the jawbones of pigs, coal, beer, porpoise teeth, hard candy, fish bones, and the red scalps of woodpeckers.

○ In 1833 Robert Owen, a Welsh social reformer, set up a plan in England to issue "labor notes." These were paper currency based on hours of a man's labor. The notes were in denominations of numbers of hours and were in existence for one year.

8

THE HIGH COST OF BEETLE JUICE

○ Funerals were lavish affairs in ancient Rome, similar to our weddings of today. Citizens joined together to help pay the costs; they accumulated money and wine which was dispersed among members and their families as necessary . . . an early form of insurance.

○ The cost of Columbus's discovery of America was about $7,000. The money for the trip was obtained by a loan using Queen Isabella's jewels as collateral.

○ Paul Revere's ride to New York to report the Boston Tea Party cost 14 pounds 2 shillings. The expense account was signed by John Hancock.

○ George Washington's expenses for winning the American Revolutionary War came to about $91,000.

○ Button Gwinnett, one of the men who signed the Declaration of Independence, died in a duel a year after the signing. Only forty known Gwinnett autographs exist, and today, this autograph is the rarest of all the Declaration signers, worth more than $100,000.

○   The highest price paid for written words was probably the approximately $2,225 a word paid for a copy of the Gettysburg Address written by Abraham Lincoln, containing ten sentences and 269 words.

○   The 1856 British Guiana one-cent magenta postage stamp is the world's most valuable stamp. It is worth more than $850,000.

○   A man named William T. Robey bought a sheet of a hundred 24-cent airmail stamps at a Washington D.C. post office in 1910. When he discovered the airplane on the stamps had been printed upside down, he sold the stamps to a dealer for $15,000. A week later, the stamps were sold again for $20,000. Today, each of those 24-cent stamps is worth more than $100,000.

○ In the same year, a baseball card was printed with the picture of Pittsburgh Pirates player Honus Wagner on it and placed in cigarette packages. Wagner, a nonsmoker, objected to having his picture appear in a promotion for cigarettes, and the cards were withdrawn, but a few remained in circulation. Today, one of the twenty-four known cards is worth more than $20,000.

○ Baseball cards started out as promotional gimmicks included in cigarette packs, but in 1931, gum companies thought of packing baseball cards with their penny packs of newly invented bubble gum. What started as a hobby, collecting the cards, is now a million-dollar industry.

○ The average bride spends between $4,000 and $5,000 on her wedding. She buys the gown, food and drink for guests, gifts for the bridegroom and bridesmaids, photographs, and limousine. The groom is expected to pay for rings, marriage license, flowers, gifts for the bride and the men in the wedding party, the clergyman's fee, and the honeymoon.

○   The original Model T Ford was more expensive ($850) than a Cadillac ($750).

○   In 1929 the price of admission to a movie was about thirty-five cents. Sixty years later it cost $7.50 to buy a ticket, or more than twenty-one times the original price.

○ The most valuable comic book is Marvel Comics No. 1, which cost a dime when it first came out in 1939 and is now worth more than $18,000.

○ In Virginia, it was once illegal for a bridegroom to pay a minister less than a dollar.

○ In 1939 the average annual income was $2,000. A television set cost 25 percent of that, $500.

○ In 1940 you could buy almost nine quarts of milk for a dollar.

○ The penny gumball now costs more than a nickel to produce.

○   A quarter to a third of an audience's money in a movie theater goes for refreshments.

○   Americans spend four times as much money on pet food as they do on baby food.

○   The territory of Alaska was purchased from the Russians in 1867 for only two cents an acre.

○   In 1988, a Saudi Arabian collector paid $7,480,000 for a flawless 52.59-carat emerald-cut white diamond.

○ The ruby slippers worn by Judy Garland in *The Wizard of Oz* were bought by an anonymous collector at an auction in 1988, making the size 6B shoes the world's highest priced pair.

○ The most expensive toy in the world is probably a dollhouse created by Neville Wilkinson that took him fifteen years to complete. The house contains sixteen rooms and 2,000 miniature works of art, as well as a guest book signed by Shirley Temple. It was purchased for $265,500 by the owners of "Legoland," a family theme park in Billund, Denmark. The dollhouse is on display there.

○ On May 15, 1990, Vincent Van Gogh's portrait of his friend, Doctor Paul Ferdinand Gachet, painted six weeks before the artist's death, drew a record $82.5 million at an auction at Christy's in New York.

○ Raising a child to age seventeen will cost the average American parents more than $55,000.

○ The most expensive condiment in the world is Ca Cuong, a secretion produced by beetles in North Vietnam, which costs a hundred dollars an ounce.

9

MILLIONAIRES AND MISERS

○ One of the most ruthless businessmen of all time was the wealthy Marcus Licinus Crassus of ancient Rome. Among the services he provided was a fire brigade which rushed to burning buildings, then waited around until Crassus exacted his price from the owner of the property before they would attempt to save it.

○ In medieval times, doctors sometimes gilded pills to make them more acceptable to wealthy customers.

○ Millionaire Cornelius Vanderbilt of New York started out going into business for himself at the age of sixteen by buying a small boat and ferrying people from Staten Island to New York City.

○ Andrew Carnegie worked as a millhand at the age of twelve for $1.20 an hour. Later, he sold his steel company for half a billion dollars.

○ John Jacob Astor, who was the wealthiest man in America, did not believe in philanthropy. Even after he made his fortune, he lived like a poor shopkeeper. He did leave $400,000 in his will to establish public libraries in New York City, but that was only after another wealthy individual, Joseph Cogswell, badgered him into it.

○ Philanthropist John D. Rockefeller gave away half of his fortune. He made his first charitable contribution at the age of sixteen and by the time he died, at eighty-two, he had given away $531,326,842.

○ Rockefeller used to carry dimes around with him to give away, usually to start a conversation about thrift.

○ Financier J. P. Morgan once attended a Senate Banking and Currency Inquiry with a female midget on his lap. Some promotion people for Ringling Brothers, Barnum & Bailey Circus had plunked her there, and the dour gentleman was so surprised and touched that he smiled and said, "I have a grandson bigger than you." The picture of the smiling tycoon changed his public image from then on to that of a kindly old gentleman.

○ Hetty Howland Green, considered the greatest woman financier in history at the time of her death in 1916, left an estate estimated at around $100 million. The stories about her unwillingness to part with her money are hair-raising, including one account that her son went without medical treatment while she looked for a free clinic, resulting in the loss of his leg.

○ An old prospector named Henry Comstock, known in Nevada as "Old Pancake," discovered the biggest U.S. silver bonanza ever found: the Comstock Lode, worth over $500 million. Comstock sold his right to it for a fortune at that time: $11,000.

○ Daisy Alexander, heiress to the Singer sewing machine fortune, wrote out a will, stuck it in a bottle, and threw it into the River Thames in London. She died two years later. Ten years after her death, an unemployed restaurant worker, Jack Wurm, noticed a bottle in the sand as he walked along the beach in San Francisco. It had a message inside. The

paper willed the finder of the message to receive half
of Daisy's fortune, which amounted to about $6 mil-
lion, and the other half to go to her lawyer, "share
and share alike."

○ The youngest person to earn a million dollars
was child film star Shirley Temple, who had accumulated wealth estimated at a million dollars before
she was ten years old.

○ Billionaire Jean Paul Getty retired at the age of
twenty-four after making his first million dollars. It
is said that Getty kept a pay phone in his mansion.

○ John F. Kennedy, the wealthiest president the
United States has ever had, received a birthday gift
from his father on his twenty-first birthday of a one-
million-dollar trust fund.

○ You cannot even place a bid for the world's largest uncut gem, the 970-carat Star of Sierra Leone, unless you can prove that you own at least $2½ million.

○ One of America's greatest fortunes, that of the Stern family, was built on birdseed. They own the Hartz Mountain Corporation, which specializes in pet foods and accessories.

○ There are a million millionaires in the world.

○ There are forty-nine billionaires in the world today, but there is some controversy over who is the single richest person. If national rulers are included, the Sultan of Brunei is the richest man; if they are excluded, Japanese railroad executive Yoshiaki Tsutsumi may have the honor of the richest person.

○ The Sultan of Brunei lives in a $300 million palace bigger than the Vatican in Rome.

○ The world's richest woman is Queen Elizabeth II of England, who is worth $7.4 billion.

○ The richest American is said to be Sam Moore Walton, of Bentonville, Arkansas, founder of Wal-Mart discount stores. Although he can afford a chauffeured limousine, Walton prefers to drive his own pickup truck.

○ Robert McCulloch, who made his fortune as the creator of McCulloch's chain saws, bought London Bridge for $2,400,000 and then had it transported, stone by stone, from its place across the Thames River in London, where it had stood for hundreds of years, to Arizona, where it is now the second most popular tourist attraction in Arizona (first is the Grand Canyon).

○ King Fahd of Saudi Arabia, worth about $20 billion, lost half a million dollars in one night of gambling on the French Riviera. An Italian industrialist lost $1,920,000 in only five hours at the roulette table in Monte Carlo, Monaco.

○ When Thomas Jefferson was president, great wealth was considered to be $300,000. Today, you cannot make *Forbes* magazine's list of the 400 richest Americans unless you have at least $225 million.

10

TAXES AND OTHER AGGRAVATIONS

○   The earliest document dealing with money was a "bill" inscribed in clay from ancient Babylonia, about 5,000 years old. It showed what a buyer owed to a merchant in exchange for goods.

○   Rabelais, the fifteenth-century satirist, said in his will: "I have nothing, I owe a great deal; the rest I give to the poor."

○   In his will, William Shakespeare left his wife his second best bed.

○   In 1695, a window tax was levied in England on all houses which had six or more windows.

○   Czar Peter I of Russia ordered all men to shave off their beards. Those who refused had to pay a fine, which became known as "beard money." Some say the law was declared because the czar could not grow a beard himself.

○   George Washington's mother was a real nag. She complained all the time, despite the fact that her famous son took very good care of her. She even petitioned Virginia's General Assembly for a public pension to prevent her from starving.

○ In early nineteenth-century America, people who could not pay their debts were often thrown into debtors' prison. Not only could a person in jail not raise any funds, but he was responsible for his own food, fuel, and clothing while he was imprisoned. Many owed no more than ten dollars.

○ A book borrowed from the University of Cincinnati Medical Library in 1823 was returned in 1968 by the borrower's great-grandson. The fine was calculated at $22,646.

○ The FBI was once brought in to break up a ring of comic book forgers. An avid collector from Cambridge, Massachusetts, traded several expensive comic books for one rare Eerie No. 1, only to suspect later that it was a fake. It turned out not to be counterfeit after all, but one of three different legitimate versions of the book.

○   Employees steal over $100 billion a year in goods, including pencils and paper clips, from their employers each year.

○   The Internal Revenue Service estimates an annual average of about $100 billion is lost through tax evasion.

○   About 99 percent of the crimes committed in the United States have to do with money or sex, and those committed for money outrank sex crimes by four to one.

○ The annual profits of organized crime are about $50 billion.

○ Norwegians pay the highest taxes in the world. Some people pay even more in taxes than they have received as income. One shipping magnate had to pay a tax bill that was for 491 percent of his income.

○ A New York woman holds the world's record for the worst scofflaw. She collected parking tickets totalling more than $200,000 in fines.

○ After an applicant for a hunting license in West Germany completes a one-hundred-hour classroom course—including doing home study, passing a three-hour oral and a three-hour written exam, and performing shooting tests—and shows proof that he carries heavy liability and property-damage insurance, he must still pay hundreds of dollars for the license.

○ The records show that crime in twentieth-century America increased during periods of prosperity and declined during hard times.

○ A Scotsman named McAllister provided for his two daughters by leaving them their weight in one-pound bank notes. The plumper of the two received about $30,000 more than her sister.

○   A woman in England left £70 for the care and maintenance of her pet goldfish, describing them as "... one is bigger than the other two, and these latter are to be easily recognized, as one is fat and the other lean." She requested also that flowers be placed upon their graves when they died.

○   The longest will on record was that of Mrs. Frederick Cook, the American widow of a British drapery manufacturer. The will was 95,940 words long, bound in four volumes, explaining how she wanted her fortune of $100,000 distributed.

○   American taxes were once used to finance a study of the blood groups of Polish pigs.

○   If you earn more than $400 in one year babysit-
ting, you have to file an income tax form with the
U.S. government.

About the Author

Barbara Seuling is the author-illustrator of many freaky facts books including *Elephants Can't Jump & Other Freaky Facts About Animals, You Can't Sneeze & Other Freaky Facts About the Human Body,* and *The Man in the Moon is Upside Down in Argentina & Other Freaky Facts About Geography.* Ms. Seuling lives most of the year in New York City.